The Lord's prayer

Matthew 6:9-13

Melody Lafferty

AuthorHouse™
1663 Liberty Drive
Bloomington, IN 47403
www.authorhouse.com
Phone: 833-262-8899

This book is printed on acid-free paper.

ISBN: 978-1-6655-5810-5 (sc)
ISBN: 978-1-6655-5811-2 (e)

Library of Congress Control Number: 2022907966

Print information available on the last page.

Published by AuthorHouse 04/26/2022

author HOUSE®

The Lords Prayer

Matthew 6:9-13

Our Father, who art in heaven,

Hallowed be thy name,

Thy kingdom come

3

Thy will be done

4

On earth

as it is in heaven

Give us this day our daily bread.

And Forgive us our trespasses,

8

As we forgive those that
trespass against us.

And Lead us not into temptation,

For thine Is the kingdom,

The power and the glory,

Forever and ever,

14

Amen.

Printed in the United States
by Baker & Taylor Publisher Services